CONTENTS

Published By Century Books Limited,
Unit 1, Upside Station Building,
Solcbro Road, Torquay, Devon, TQ2 6FD
books@centurybooksltd.co.uk Published 2011

THE SATURDAYS

£7.99

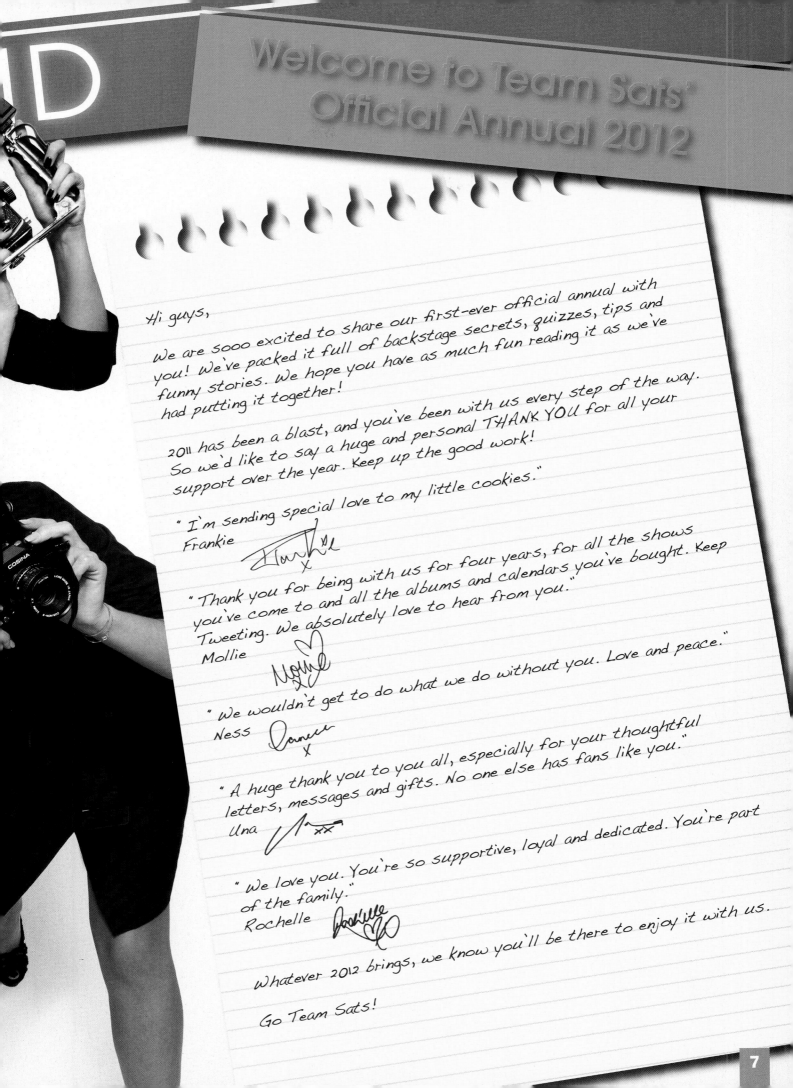

Hi guys,

We are sooo excited to share our first-ever official annual with you! We've packed it full of backstage secrets, quizzes, tips and funny stories. We hope you have as much fun reading it as we've had putting it together!

2011 has been a blast, and you've been with us every step of the way. So we'd like to say a huge and personal THANK YOU for all your support over the year. Keep up the good work!

"I'm sending special love to my little cookies."
Frankie
X

"Thank you for being with us for four years, for all the shows you've come to and all the albums and calendars you've bought. Keep Tweeting. We absolutely love to hear from you."
Mollie

"We wouldn't get to do what we do without you. Love and peace."
Ness
X

"A huge thank you to you all, especially for your thoughtful letters, messages and gifts. No one else has fans like you."
Una

"We love you. You're so supportive, loyal and dedicated. You're part of the family."
Rochelle

Whatever 2012 brings, we know you'll be there to enjoy it with us.

Go Team Sats!

FRANKIE

Frankie Sandford

Age: 22

Home town: Upminster

Pets: Two dogs – Presley and Pixie

Phobias: Ketchup – yuck yuck yuck!

Weirdest fan gift: A wedding ring

Best Christmas pressie: A dolls' house

Would most like to work with: Rihanna

Fave band: Paramore

Most embarrassing moment:

Probably when I tripped on GMTV during one of our first-ever performances. I'm always tripping over. There's a Youtube bloopers reel someone's made and posted online – a compilation of my finest falls.

"Frankie's honest."

Mollie

"Frankie is straight up."

Vanessa

MOLLIE

Mollie King

Age: 24

Home town: Wandsworth

Fave fan gift: Books of pics of my dog Alfie

On my iPod: John Mayer, High School Musical soundtrack, loads of Britney Spears, Regina Spektor, Paolo Nutini

Guilty pleasure: Chocolate

Pets: Poodle

Fave dog breed: Golden Retriever

Greatest fear: Flying – I get sweaty palms and start shaking, especially when there's turbulence over the Atlantic. I can't get my head around how the thing stays in the air at all.

"Mollie is just lovely and very generous."

Frankie

"Mollie is smiley."

Una

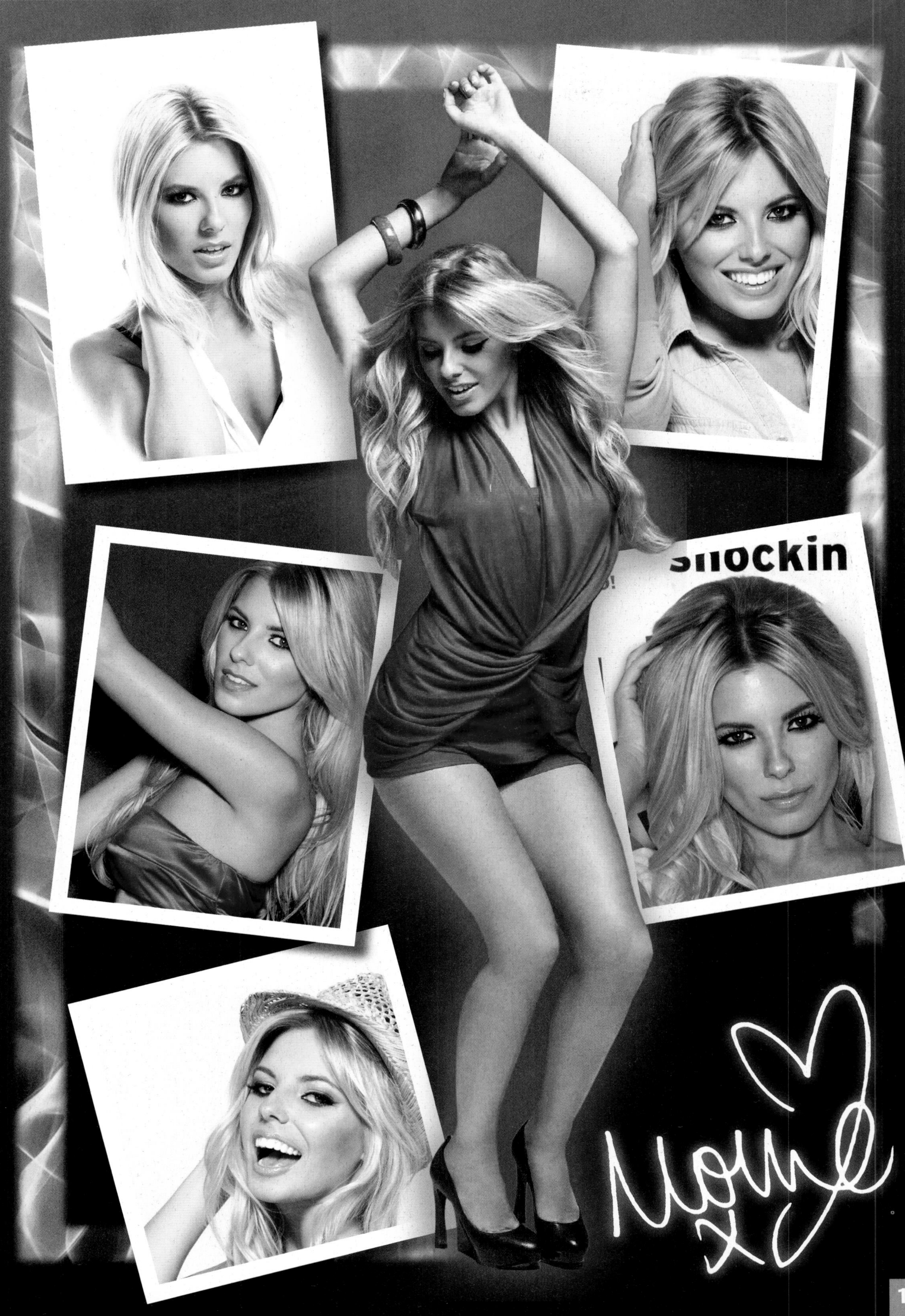

ROCHELLE

Rochelle Wiseman

Age: 22

Home town: Barking

Pets: Tiger, a Yorkshire Terrier

Guilty pleasure: Watching old episodes of Come Dine With Me and eating chocolate eclairs and chicken korma!

Fave fan gift: Fan books containing pics we might not have seen

Fave food: I've recently discovered I love cockles!

On my iPod: Cover Drive

Hobby: I love doing really, really hard jigsaw puzzles. There's one called Wozzajig, where you have to guess what the people on the front of the box are looking at and then do the jigsaw showing what they see. It's well difficult!

"Rochelle is a proper little housewife." Frankie

" Rochelle is caring." Mollie

UNA

Una Healy

Age: 29

Home town: Thurles, Republic of Ireland

Guilty pleasure: Tea

Pets: Cats, dogs and terrapins

Fave Sats tracks: 'Ego' and 'Higher'

Fave film genre: Comedy

Signature dish: I can make amazing brown soda bread from a recipe passed down through my family.

Most embarrassing moment: On our first tour I had a nightmare with a chainmail top – its skinny straps broke so I had to do half a routine with it hanging off me!

Greatest fear: I absolutely hate spiders. I often wake up thinking they're all over my face. It was really embarrassing once when I was sharing with Vanessa when this happened. I woke her up screaming they were all over me.

"Una takes ten minutes to say something she could have said in two words!" Vanessa

"Una is a party animal and night owl. She is very intelligent and knows something about everything." Rochelle

VANESSA

Vanessa White

Age: 21

Home town: Stratford

Onstage experience: The King and I and The Lion King

Style icons: Vanessa Hudgens, Kim Kardashian, J-Lo

Fave fan gift: A really nice T-shirt

Worst trait: Messy and scatty!

Pets: Two dogs – George and Peaches

Fave artists of 2011: Frank Ocean, The Weekend, Marsha Ambrosius

Guilty pleasure: True Blood

Signature dish: I don't really know how to cook any proper meals. But recently I cooked a Thai green curry for some friends and I don't like to boast but it was a-mazing! In fact it was so good no one believed I'd made it myself. They thought I'd had my mum round to prepare it for me!

"Vanessa is so cheeky and hilarious to be around. She can't stop cracking jokes!" Rochelle

Check out these fab snaps from the set of the awesome video for 'Higher'. It was shot at Fox Studios in L.A. on a set made to look like a New York street. Everyone who's anyone has filmed there, from Britney Spears to Chris Brown . . . and now Team Sats!

Here's Tyler the director checking my manicure." *Mollies*

"We felt like we were in Sex and The City – ignore the rollers and tracksuits!" *Mollie*

Quick touch up!" *Frankie*

"It was great to work with such a talented crew." *Vanessa*

"The look was more relaxed and playful than usual." *Mollie*

"We were all in a cheeky mood on the day of the shoot!" *Una*

"Having my hair in a ponytail was a big change and meant I was cooler in the hot sun." *Vanessa*

"This shot sums up our day. It was like a girlie summer holiday. So much fun." *Vanessa*

Gotta look your best at ll times in L.A. just in ase you bump into Zac fron!" *Mollie*

"We were really lucky with the weather - it was incredible all day" *Rochelle*

"Yes, that's us inside the cool vintage car!" *Una*

19

"As well as the fab car we had an old-skool yellow school bus on set." *Mollie*

"I had to dance on the boot of the taxi. I was terrified I'd fall through." *Rochelle*

"We're hands-on and keep tabs on progress. We all loved this video straight off." *Rochelle*

"I loved my outfit, especially the red boots – I can't wait to wear them again." *Una*

"I didn't like any of the clothes initially so the director took me out shopping for this fab dress from Urban Outfitters." *Frankie*

"Lining up for a shot. We really felt we were living the dream." *Mollie*

We had a blast shooting this vid and it's definitely one of our faves. We heart L.A.

The Sats xxxx

QUIZ PART 1 – TEST YOURSELF!

Just how much do you know about your favourite girl band? Answer the questions below and keep a note of your score. There are five parts to this quiz, so record your scores as you go and find out whether you can keep up with The Saturdays!

1. What is the name of The Saturdays' debut album?

2. Which Saturdays' song was the Comic Relief single in 2009?

3. Which girl is the eldest band member?

4. What is the name of The Saturdays' record label?

5. What is the name of The Saturdays' first single?

6. Which band is member comes from The Republic of Ireland?

7. 'Just Can't Get Enough' is a cover of a song by which 80s' band?

8. Which American rapper and singer featured on the single 'Higher'?

9. What is the name of the reality TV show that filmed The Saturdays' in 2010?

10. Which girl's home town is Barking?

Released 28 July 2008
1. If This Is Love
2. What Am I Gonna Do?

Released 13 October 2008
1. Up
2. Crashing Down

Released 5 January 2009
1. Issues
2. Beggin'

Released 29 June 2009
1. Work
2. Unofficial

Released 5 October 2009
1. Forever Is Over
2. I Can't Wait

Released 3 January 2010
1. Ego
2. Flashback

Released 5 August 2010
1. Missing You
2. Ready to Rise

Released 1 November 2010
1. Higher Feat. Flo Rida
2. Had It With Today

Released 22 May 2011
1. Notorious
2. Not That Kinda Girl

Released 4 September 2011
1. All Fired Up
2. Ladykiller

Released 2 March 2009
1. Just Can't Get Enough
2. Golden Rules

Released 27 October 2008
Chasing Lights
1. If This is Love
2. Up
3. Keep Her
4. Issues
5. Lies
6. Work
7. Chasing Lights
8. Set Me Off
9. Fall
10. Vulnerable
11. Why Me, Why Now
12. Just Can't Get Enough
13. Up (Wideboys Remix Edit)

Released 12 October 2009
Wordshaker
1. Forever is Over
2. Here Standing
3. Ego
4. No One
5. One Shot
6. Wordshaker
7. Denial
8. Open Up
9. Lose Control
10. Not Good Enough
11. Deeper
12. 2 A.M.

Released 16 August 2010
Headlines
1. Missing You
2. Ego
3. Higher
4. Forever Is Over
5. Died In Your Eyes
6. Karma
7. Puppet
8. One Shot (Starsmith Mix)
9. Here Standing
10. Lose Control
11. Deeper
12. Higher Feat. Flo Rida

Backstage Pass on the Headline Tour!
Following the release of their spectacular album Headlines, the Saturdays headed out on a massive tour at the start of 2011. They hit twenty of the UK's coolest cities, and the fans went wild! Now you can find out what the best girl band in the land thought of their live show . . .

"I loved the fact we got to go back to Ireland." *Una*

"Touring's my favourite part of being in a band." *Frankie*

"We couldn't wait to get onstage." *Mollie*

"Touring is quite scary." *Vanessa*

"Every night of a tour is a stand out moment." *Rochelle*

"We had about four outfits on this tour and I remember panicking before each change. You're always scared you won't get into your next outfit in time."

"One night our tour manager Mark ran on stage and did ballet leaps around while we were trying to perform. He loves a prank!"

"Hammersmith was my favourite date and also the hardest. It was amazing because it's my old stomping ground."

"I love our pre-show ritual. Before we go on stage we always do the Sats Hi Five. Sometimes we'll give each other a pep talk and wish each other luck."

"Knowing that people have paid for tickets and are wanting to make you their night out is a huge compliment."

"I like travelling between venues, seeing the countryside. We don't have a tour bus; we have cars so we chat and read. When we're backstage we're either chilling out in catering, having our hair and make-up done or chatting. But right before each show on the tour we always get quiet – probably due to the nerves."

"Our fans are unique. They are very loyal and protective of us, and they are so varied in age groups. We're always surprised to see everyone from very young girls to women in their forties, groups of teenages and guys. It's great."

"The first time doing the whole set with costume changes, we had three minutes to run off stage, change and come back. The problem was that we were taking nine minutes! The tour manager was horrified. In the end we spent all afternoon just taking our clothes off and on, off and on. But by the end of the tour we'd got it down to just sixty seconds!"

"I particularly loved playing Liverpool and Manchester because I have family up north and I felt at home up there. I love the North! But London will always be my heartland. The whole tour was one big laugh. We're like a family and we just kid about all the time."

"We did Belfast and Dublin, which was really special for me coz all my friends and family got to see us. My uncle Declan Nerney – a famous country singer – came one night. He inspired me to get into music and has been a huge encouragement. It really meant a lot to me when he said he was blown away by our show. For him to say that was hue."

THE SATURDAYS

ALL FIRED UP!

DECEMBER

FRIDAY   02
BOURNEMOUTH BIC

SATURDAY   03
LIVERPOOL ECHO ARENA

MONDAY   05
CARDIFF MOTORPOINT ARENA

TUESDAY   06
BRIGHTON CENTRA

THURSDAY   08
BIRMINGHAM LG ARENA

FRIDAY   09
MANCHESTER MEN ARENA

SATURDAY   10
NEWCASTLE METRO RADIO ARENA

MONDAY   12
NOTTINGHAM CAPITAL FM ARENA

TUESDAY   13
GLASGOW SICC

THURSDAY   15
SHEFFIELD MOTORPOINT ARENA

FRIDAY   16
LONDON WEMBLEY ARENA

SUNDAY   18
BELFAST ODYSSEY ARENA

MONDAY   19
DUBLIN O2

"I had really bad hair.
I cut it myself and dyed
one side yellow."

FRANKIE

Grab a few minutes for a natter with Frankie about pets, Posh Spice and popcorn . . .

What's your biggest beauty mistake?
I went through an 'Emo' phase shortly before I joined the band and I had really bad hair. I cut it myself and dyed one side yellow and the other black, and put in long black extensions! Nice!

Are you a red carpet girl at heart?
Although I love getting glammed up, I am really outdoorsy at heart. I love slumming it on camping trips. When I was younger I used to love doing this assault course thing called 'Stubbers' in Essex. I'm surprisingly good at clambering up things.

You have a pug and a Chihuahua – are you planning to get any more dogs?
I like big dogs, but they're not portable. When I get older I might have one though. I can't take Presley and Pixie everywhere, but sometimes I take them on photo shoots and recently we did something for the Dog's Trust so they came along then. My parents live near me so they look after them if I'm away.

You've been working pretty hard this year – have you had time for a holiday?
I recently went away with Mollie and it was lovely – when you spend as much time as we do together you can be at ease and fine with silence.

So who's your ideal holiday partner?
Obviously I like holidaying with my boyfriend! When I was in my teens I found the thought of holidaying with family dreadful but now I'm like 'Mum, Dad, can I come with you?'

What's your fave type of holiday?
I like to be on a beach. I want to step out on a balcony and see the sea, otherwise it doesn't seem like a holiday. Ideally I'd have about three a year. I would have skiing hols, a fun adventurous holiday (maybe Richard Branson's tree safari place in Africa) and a lazy sunbathing holiday!

Obviously being in The Sats is a dream come true, but if you could be in any other band, which one would you choose?
Spice Girls, hands down. They were pioneers and it looked so much fun – new and fresh. The clothes were just outrageous!

So come on, spill, which Spice Girl did you want to be?
Posh, definitely! I was totally starstruck when I met her while in S Club Juniors.

If you weren't in The Saturdays what would you be doing?
I'd be an English teacher. English was my favourite subject at school and I was considering a career in teaching before I joined the Saturdays.

Which was your fave tour date?
Hammersmith was the most amazing venue. We were filming the DVD at the same time so we did two shows. It was a jam-packed day because we had our most meet-and-greets ever, plus a load of press to do for Germany, but the show was awesome. Often the dates up North are better than in London as the crowds are louder and more lively, but this was just amazing.

So what's in your backstage rider – are you secretly total divas?
Our rider has been pretty dull! We did have nuts, fruit, lemon and honey for our throats. Now we've added things like face wipes and salted popcorn, but it's still not very rock and roll. We don't wash our hair in bottled water!

Has anything ever gone wrong during a live show?
There are always things that go wrong on tour! In the Headlines tour we had these big screens at the back which were supposed to open and then we'd come through, but they kept getting jammed shut. We also had really steep stairs to come down. They were really wobbly and we nearly tripped in our high heels, so in the end they had to add banisters so we could hold on!

"There are always things that go wrong on tour!"

THE SATURDAYS ON EACH OTHER!

"In Mollie's life everything's a big fairy tale – she wants her prince and palace."

"Frankie calls herself sunshine and showers – she's either embracing everything or she's quiet."

"Rochelle is the biggest chatterbox."

The Sats have plenty to say for themselves, but what happened when we asked what they really think about each other? Read on for the inside scoop!

"Vanessa is cheeky!"

"Una makes us laugh and says it how it is."

"Frankie is amazingly honest."

"Mollie is always upbeat. We call her Miss Disney!"

"Vanessa is definitely free-spirited."

"Una knows herself and sticks to her guns."

"Rochelle is like a big sister."

QUIZ PART 2 - IT'S ALL IN THE LYRICS

So you think you know The Saturdays? Just how closely do you listen to their lyrics?
Test yourself, then carry your score forward to the next challenge...

1. 'So when I speak listen cause you keep on pushing like I need permission to be heard . . .'

2. 'If you lose me then you know, you're just a bit too slow . . .'

3. 'You know I like it in the street lights, like I like the spotlight . . .'

4. 'I got the goods and I want you, put your boots on baby get to . . .'

5. 'Are you standing by my window when I'm asleep . . . .'

6. 'I don't think you know where your head is . . .'

7. 'Can't decide if I should leave you or kiss you . . .'

8. 'You're like an angel and you give me your love . . .'

9. 'I get high when you're making me weak . . .'

10. 'I wish I could turn back the page
Re-write my point of view . . .'

EGO   ROCHELLE   STYLE
FRANKIE   SATURDAYS   TOUR
ISSUES   SINGLE   UNA
MOLLIE   STARDOM   VANESSA
NOTORIOUS   STUDIO   VIDEO

```
V A N E S S A R O M O D R U S
I U R O C A V E L Y T S Y A N
D E C I S T Y L R D O M T U O
E S E L L U F G A N U U M N T
T O U R E H R U N S S R O D T R
S A K O A D L I E D S S U R I
A M O D R A T S V E T S N D O
T D E R O Y D A I S G M O A U
O I D U T S T K D E L O T Y S
M S O N O D N I L L H E K A J
I S M A M A V I S R H L S S A
D U A S R N T M O L L I E T R
E E O F I O D R A T M A T O U
O S U K C V A N E S A R K M V
S A S E R O C H E L L E T S I
```

40

Filmed in April 2011, the music video for 'Notorious' was the group's second to be shot in Los Angeles. James Larese of L.A.-based directing trio Syndrome was at the helm, having directed for major artists including Kesha, Alicia Keys, Eminem, The Black Eyed Peas and Estelle. The fab film features the girls nine-to-fiving as secretaries before heading off out to partay!

"I ate bags of crunchy Cheetos that day – not good for the lippy!" *Frankie*

"This is us walking from our trailers to the set. The trailers have everything from fridges and TVs to beds!" *Rochelle*

"There was this really cool guy there who whipped us up and got us in the mood for the party scenes, we were like 'can we take him with us?'" *Vanessa*

"Phew – a moment off the high heels!" *Una*

"Say cheese, girls!" *Mollie*

"I'm a gangsta on the dance floor!" *Frankie*

"This is actually in an empty furniture store – the next room was piled high with sofas." *Frankie*

"I used to work as a secretary, but I never looked this glam." *Una*

"I loved the fact we had roles to play."
Rochelle

"This is absolutely my fave vid – it's a great story and very polished and classy." *Mollie*

THE SATURDAYS "NOTORIOUS"
J. LARESE   "12 FPS"   A-CAM
Y. THOMAS   4.7.11

"These days the clapboards aren't like blackboards and are too expensive for us to keep!" *Rochelle*

Will someone please answer that phone!

"Aww! We had super-cute Saturday's stamps!" *Mollie*

"I'd make an awful secretary – I really needed direction! " *Vanessa*

You've been Saturday'd!

"Our manager came up with the idea of us as secretaries but Mollie came up with the lift and nightclub concepts. She's very creative." *Una*

James has worked with so many hip-hop artists we thought, 'he's not gonna get the Saturdays' – but he was amazing." *Mollie*

"I used to hate red lipstick but our make-up team have persuaded me it's fierce." *Vanessa*

"Which way to the partay?" *Una*

It's a wrap!

"I jumped out of a plane with the red devils last year"

UNA

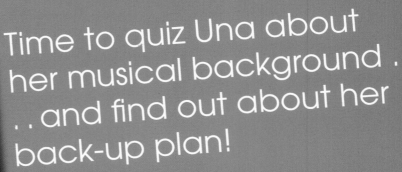

Time to quiz Una about her musical background . . . and find out about her back-up plan!

What did you do before you going into music?
Loads of things! I left school at seventeen and trained for a year in business management. Then I went on to work as a medical secretary. I was good at it as I am very organised. I'm still like that! I worked in an office until I was twenty-one. Then I decided that I wanted to do music, and focused more on that. But I also trained for a while as a nurse and primary school teacher.

You like to keep busy, don't you!
I was trying to find a back-up plan in case the singing didn't work out. Dad is a doctor and Mum is a nurse. I gave up nursing aged twenty-two to give the singing a go. Mum and Dad were totally behind me.

How did you make your dream a reality?
I bought a PA system and started playing clubs and bars and pubs, I'd play guitar, doing covers and crowd pleasers. I'd often team up with another girl. I gigged at weekends.

What did you play?
I did everything from The Eagles to Bryan Adams, and turned 'Toxic' into an acoustic song. The set list depended on the crowd.

What did you gain from that time?
I have an authentic music background. It was a great experience. I'd sometimes play for just four or five people, which could be soul destroying, but I loved people coming who were obviously really listening to my music.

Have you always written your own songs?
When I did my GCSE equivalent exams back home in Ireland I took music and I performed my own composition. I got a grade A! When I was gigging I was writing a lot of music, which was always in back of head.

What do you like doing in your spare time?
I love going to the cinema. I've got to catch up on the Harry Potters – I've only seen the first film. I jumped out of a plane with the Red Devils last year. I bought it as a present for my boyfriend, but I did it with him – even though I'm scared of heights. I was so proud of myself!

Frankie and Mollie went on holiday together this year, and so did Rochelle and Vanessa. What did you get up to?
Yes, I haven't holidayed with the girls apart from L.A. This year we had a week off so I spent time with Ben while the other girls went away. But we socialise a lot outside of work. We're good friends and we like to have something to talk about besides work, so this means we can talk about what happened last night! We go for nice food and then go out dancing. We're big, big dancers.

So who rules the dance floor?
I'd never have been first on the dance floor, but with the girls you just can't be a wallflower. It's so much fun – Vanessa's got some great moves. When she lets loose she winds and moves and is so flexible. She looks amazing.

If you weren't in The Saturdays what would you be doing?
I always thought I should have a back-up plan in case the music didn't work out. Maybe I'd keep nursing in the family!

"I love going to the cinema."

DID YOU KNOW...

Vanessa grew up in the same neighbourhood as Jade from the Sugababes.

Una was a bit of a swot at school! Her fave subjects were biology and home economics.

Breakfast is Mollie's fave meal of the day.

Una used t
guinea pig

Mollie is a huge worrier.

Vanessa's totally hooked on the TV series *True Blood*.

Mollie adores Britney Spears and has been to every tour!

Frankie used to be a Brownie. She was once awarded the 'Best Little Monkey' certificate for being the quickest to the top of the climbing wall.

Rochelle chills out by going on drives around the countryside.

ed

Frankie's guilty pleasure is a fishing programme called *Deadliest Catch!*

Rochelle loves doing brain-scramblingly hard jigsaw puzzles!

One of the Sats doubles up as a pet heroine! Vanessa recently saved her dog Peaches from a hungry fox.

QUIZ PART 3 – MOVING PICTURES!

So you know the facts and you've listened to the lyrics, but just how closely have you watched The Saturdays' videos? Answer the questions below and don't forget to carry your score forward.

1. Which video starts with the girls in a lift, going to work in an office block?

2. The girls get out of a New York City cab in the video for which song?

3. In the video for which song do the girls wear superhero outfits?

4. Which video shows the girls on a catwalk in a warehouse?

5. Mollie looks a bit lonely as she rides her bike by the sea in the video for which song?

6. It's not all sunshine on a video shoot ... which video features the girls dealing with their problems under colourful umbrellas?

7. Which video has the girls dancing on moving pillars?

8. Can't get enough of the girls dressed up as 1950s pin-ups? Can you remember the video?

9. Which video features the girls cheering themselves up with a popcorn fight?

10. The girls are adored by screaming fans as they perform in a shop window in which video?

"I was really naughty at school!"

VANESSA

Join Vanessa on the couch for a cosy chat!

You're all well known for your individual styles and looks. What happens if two of you want to wear the same outfit?
We never squabble over clothes, maybe coz we've all got different tastes and are different body shapes. I always like what the girls wear, but I know it wouldn't look good on me. Shoes are a different story though. We all love heels. If we were the same shoe size it'd be a problem!

So how would you describe the styles of the other girls?
Una has that whole boho vibe going on, the Nicole Richie look. Mollie loves a little skirt and belt. Frankie's a jeans, vest and heels person. Rochelle loves heels and I think she looks pretty sophisticated.

What about you? How has your style developed?
We've all blossomed in the past four years. As a group we've grown and changed together. But everyone makes mistakes. Our worst was when we were all put in different coloured dresses for a premiere. They were so bad and we all agreed we looked terrible. That's our collective worst mistake. They were bespoke, made for us. We rip our stylist and he says 'I don't want to talk about it.' We looked awful!

What have you found out about yourself this year?
I didn't really enjoy being on *Popstar to Opera Star*. It was really tough and I've discovered opera definitely isn't my thing!

You've said that writing the new album has been amazing. How much of it did you write and what was the experience like?
We've done half the album and written some for the next one. We've had lots more input. I'm more creative after 12 o' clock though – I'm not a morning person! We write in twos or threes. Otherwise with five strong-minded girls there are just too many opinions flying around.

What's the toughest thing about being on tour?
I find the dances are a lot to remember, but in the end you do the moves so much they become second nature. If you overthink what you've got to do, you start forgetting bits and then you get even more scared.

If you weren't in The Saturdays what would you be doing?
I've always done music and have never wanted to do anything except sing so if I wasn't in the group I'd be trying to launch a solo career or find another band or I'd try out musical theatre.

"Opera definitely isn't my thing!"

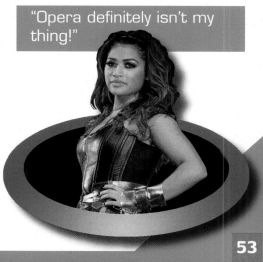

We heard that you rescued your dog from a fox recently. OMG! What happened?
She's a tiny Pomeranian cross and one evening, while I was getting ready for a night out, I let her in the garden. Next thing I hear a bark and look out to see her being dragged through a hedge by a fox! I ran out there screaming, and my neighbours came to help. The fox must have got spooked and luckily Peaches managed to escape its clutches unharmed.

What were you like at school?
I was really naughty at school! I wasn't academic at all. I went to a good school but I didn't want to have to do ballet or tap – I just wanted to sing. So I would bunk off! Everyone I went to school with was talented. I feel they're all up and coming, you don't know them yet . . . but you will.

Do you and the other girls hang out together?
Definitely! We often socialise and go out together.

What about doing each others' hair and nails, that kind of thing?
[*Laughs*] No, we don't make each other up. In the beginning I used to help Mollie tonging her hair coz she couldn't do it. Now we all know how to do ourselves.

DESIGN A GIG POSTER!

Imagine that The Saturdays are going to play a show in your home town. You need to tell the world so that it's a sell-out gig. Use your creative skills to design a poster that has the wow factor. Use the past gig posters to inspire you. Don't forget, it's up to you to make this a success!

This slick and edgy video for the Saturday's brilliant dance track 'All Fired Up' was shot in a studio in East London. Directed by Ryan Hope, the set featured glossy black tiles that had to be polished and shone between takes and catsuit-clad dancers writhing in water. Read on to find out what happened on set . . .

"Looking fresh-faced at the ... We didn't

"The clothes for the video shoot were SO lovely - we were like kids in a candy shop!" Frankie

"Gorgeous! You'd never guess I was suffering agonising shin splints." *Vanessa*

"These dresses were much more comfortable than our boiling black leather outfits." *Mollie*

"I was the last to be shot individually. I wasn't on camera till 7pm, but it was worth the wait." *Una*

"My necklace was made out of whistles. It made my outfit edgier." *Rochelle*

dress was kind of Grecian with a of the St Frankie

"Our make-up artist Celena is always uber-prepared so her kit is massive. We love having a root through!" *Vanessa*

"There were so many looks for this vid. It was a real challenge." *Vanessa*

"There was a huge crew and I was so nervous filming my solo shots as I'm so used to being with the girls." *Mollie*

"Normally we have a plot to our videos but this was more like a beauty shoot with dancing!" *Frankie*

"There's loads of waiting around for each shot to be set up." *Una*

"This bit was filmed on a revolving turntable – I felt sick and dizzy. Frankie wanted to go faster!" *Rochelle*

"We knew the dance routine inside out but we were nervous coz we wanted to nail it." *Frankie*

"The end result is slick but we were so hot and our feet were killing us." *Vanessa*

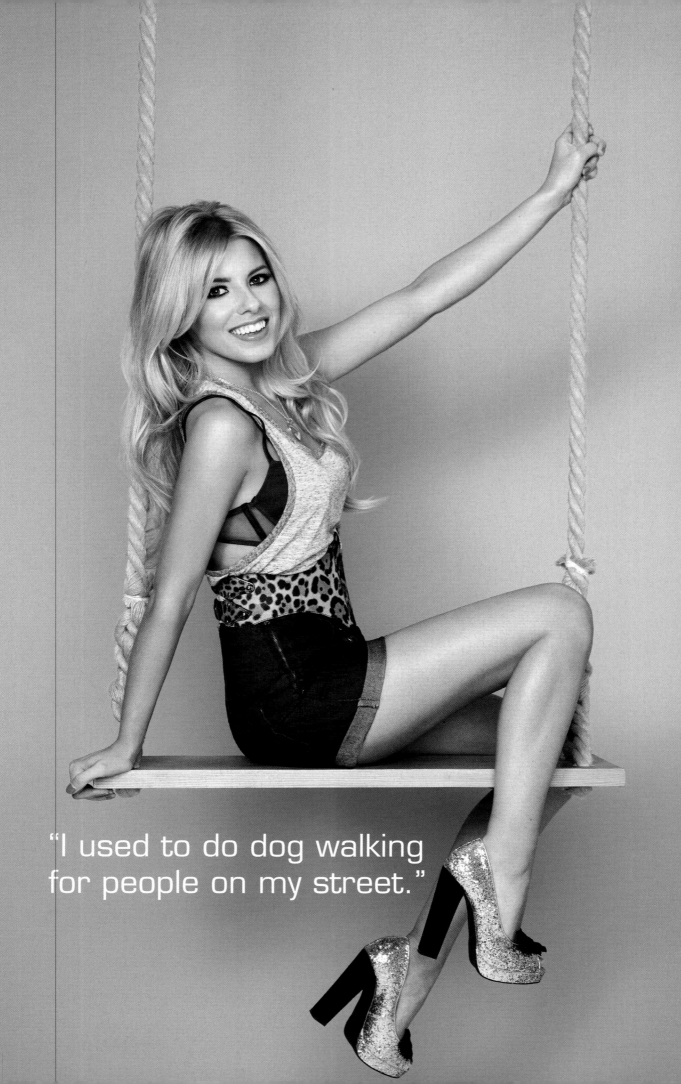

"I used to do dog walking
for people on my street."

MOLLIE

Settle down for a chat about dogs, skiing, Britney and more!

We know you love your fans – do you check out the fan forums?
Of course! Fans are reason we do this, so we have to take on board what they say, the good and the bad. Twitter makes us accessible, which is great. I look at things like what they think of the tour and our new tracks. I love it when they say we exceeded expectations!

What's your funniest tour memory?
There was one gig where the dressing room was tiny. We were all squeezed in – hair and make-up and stylists and clothes, and Frankie had brought her boyfriend! We were claustrophobic sardines. That night the screens didn't open so we had to slither through one by one, out of the tiniest gap. I remember thinking, 'This wouldn't happen to Take That!'

Is there anything you'd like to change about yourself?
I over analyse things. I worry about everything and anything. If we have an interview early on Radio 1 I will wake up every hour so as not to miss the

alarm call. And every time I crack a joke I worry if I'll offend someone. It's out of control and I need to chill out!

What's your idea of indulgence?
You can't beat a full English – I love that, a massive plateful with all the trimmings. I have to have double of each thing – two bacon slices, two eggs, two hash browns. I tend to have a big brekkie then lunch is always a snack on the go. But I have a nice, big dinner.

You've said that you love Britney Spears – tell us more . . .
I'm obsessed with Britney Spears! I'm her number-one fan. I grew up watching her in interviews – if I knew her we'd be bezzie mates. We're so similar. It's sad that she went through a horrid time, but she seems to be coming through it. She puts on the best live show!!

If you weren't in The Saturdays what would you be doing?
If I hadn't gone into The Saturdays I'd probably still be skiing. But if this all ended I might go into something with animals, maybe train as a vet.

So you're an animal lover then?
I adore dogs. When I was younger I used to do dog-walking for people on my street. I have a toy poodle called Alfie. He's much more rock-and-roll than me! He's a terrible show-off when he's around all the other Sat Pooches. We try not to bring them all along at the same time though because it's just too hectic. Alfie gets on with Presley but not Pixie. She growls at him a lot.

Have you always had dogs in your life?
We had one called Holly when I was growing up. She was so hairy and moulted everywhere, but we adored her. Having big dogs is very different from owning small ones. Big dogs become like another member of the family.

"This wouldn't happen to Take That!"

NEW ALBUM

DAYS

RADAR

WRITTEN IN THE STARS

AQUARIUS (Jan 21 – Feb 19)

Aquarians are true independent spirits. They can be a bit of a mystery and certainly don't follow the crowd, so they may surprise you!

Don't be afraid to say what you really think. You are the trendsetter of the zodiac – dare to be different!

PIECES (Feb 20 – March 20)

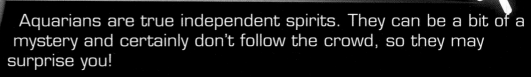

Sensitive and emotional, Pisceans are great listeners and usually make friends for life. They can be dreamers and like to escape into their imagination.

Time to let go of past regrets! Pluck up the courage to make those positive changes you're always talking about.

ARIES (March 21 – April 20)

ROCHELLE 21st March, 1989

Aries girls are often adventurous, energetic and confident.

They are good at getting what they want; sometimes they can be single-minded in pursuit of their goal. They tend to be creative people who inspire and lead others.

Expect big things from 2012! Friendships are in the stars.

Look out for new opportunities to make friends and expect your year to be full of fun.

TAURUS (April 21 – May 20)

Taureans can be stubborn. They like to know what is going on around them, otherwise they feel insecure. They make good, trustworthy friends and are generous. They like the finer things in life.

Everybody falls out with friends sometimes. Leave behind those tricky times and look forward to sunny days in 2012!

GEMINI (May 21 – June 20)

MOLLIE 4th June, 1987

Restless Geminis like to be surrounded by people.

They are social butterflies but tend to be easily bored. This makes them great company when they are in the mood, but they can also be frustrating as they are charged with nervous energy.

You've been crushing on someone for ages. Don't think they haven't noticed! Just be patient and good things will come.

# CANCER (June 21 – July 22)

Cancerians are often homebodies who like to be around their friends and families. They are emotional people who have close friends.

Trust your instincts – they never let you down! Your bosom buddies are your shinning stars – plenty of fun awaits you in 2012.

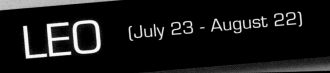

LEO (July 23 - August 22)

Proud and sometimes bossy, Leos like to be in charge and enjoy the limelight. As friends they will be generous, look after you and be the life and soul of every party.

You really know how to take the lead in 2012. Now is the time to make things happen and surge ahead with those plans of yours!

VIRGO (August 23 - Sept 22)

Virgos can be shy and cautious. They prefer friends to take the lead, and sometimes need a bit of persuasion to let their hair down. Virgos are always happiest when they are looking after their mates.

Put the worries of 2011 aside. 2012 is all about you and your dreams – now is the time to start talking to your friends and letting them know how you really feel!

LIBRA (Sept 23 - Oct 22)

UNA 10th October, 1981

Librans are chatty people who like nothing more than to be surrounded by friends or family. They are great listeners who their friends will turn to when they need help.

What's all the fuss about? You know how to handle yourself and you've got great friends to back you up. Don't let anyone take advantage of you in 2012 – this is your year to shine!

♏ SCORPIO (Oct 23 - Nov 21)

VANESSA 30th October, 1989

Scorpios are emotional, sensual creatures whose feelings run deep. They like to get things done and have no patience for hanging around. You've been feeling unnoticed lately, but that's about to change! A certain somebody knows how to make you feel like a star in 2012.

♐ SAGITTARIUS (Nov 22 - Dec 21)

Having fun is what Sagittarians are all about. They are fearless when trying new things, but don't back them into a corner – they don't like to be tied down!

Change is nothing to fear! Think of all the new opportunities coming your way. Go with the flow in 2012 and nothing will stop you.

♑ CAPRICORN (Dec 22 - Jan 20)

FRANKIE 14th January, 1989

Capricorns can see both the positive and negative sides of life. Sometimes they lack confidence and need a bit of encouragement. Then they can really let go and enjoy themselves.

Stop worrying and let your hair down!

Capricorns, you can work hard and play hard. Make sure you get that balance right in 2012!

QUIZ PART 4
BACK TO THEIR ROOTS

We all have to start somewhere. It is where we come from that makes us unique! How much do you know about The Saturdays' history?

1. Which band member auditioned for *The X Factor* in 2007 as part of girl band *Fallen Angelz?*

2. Who use to walk their neighbour's dogs when she was younger?

3. Who was a national swimming champion when she was nine?

4. Which Saturday was a professional skier?

5. Which Saturday is dyslexic?

6. Which Saturday attended the Sylvia Young Theatre School?

7. Which two girls were members of S Club Juniors?

8. Who worked as a medical secretary before joining The Saturdays?

9. Who starred in Children's TV show I Dream?

10. Who was in the West End production of *The Lion King* before joining The Saturdays?

ACROSS

2. Name the vid that the Sats filmed on a fake New York street in L.A.

4. The baby of the band.

6. In which musical did Vanessa play a character called Nala?

9. The only Gemini in the band.

10. What sign of the zodiac was Frankie born under?

12. Vanessa features on an album by Master ——

13. Who is Rochelle's biggest musical inspiration?

15. What colour is Vanessa's dress on the 'Chasing Lights' album cover?

16. Which dance troupe did the girls challenge to a dance-off on reality TV show *The Saturdays 24/7*?

18. Who directed the vid for 'All Fired Up'?

19. The girls call Mollie Miss _____.

DOWN

1. My name is Francesca but you can call me__

3. A member of S Club Juniors, alongside Frankie.

5. The name of their 2011 tour.

7. Rochelle's best friend is her__

8. The only non-English member of the band.

11. What was Vanessa like at School?

12. Rochelle's favourite activity?

14. What is Vanessa's surname?

17. Which band was Una looking forward to seeing at the V Festival 2011?

"I'd have loved to
be in Destiny's Child."

ROCHELLE

Shopaholic Rochelle spills the beans about life in the band . . .

So how was your holiday with Vanessa?
It was totally chilled. We hung out at the beach, pushed each other in the pool, that kind of thing! We did a bit of partying but not too much . . . we wanted to relax and get away from it all.

You like to escape from the pop star lifestyle occasionally, then?
Being in the goldfish bowl of fame makes me nervous. But I really feel that I belong in a band. It's everything I dreamed of when I was little, and even more.

What sort of music inspired you when you were growing up?
My mum loved Boy George and used to make me sing his songs all the time. As I got a bit older, she changed and made me sing the Fugees 'Killing Me Softly'. My mum's like me, we love pop music and we both have quite wide tastes. I'd love to have met Michael Jackson – he's been a huge inspiration to me.

How would you describe your music?
Although our sound is mainly pop, we like to bring in influences such as dance and R&B. We've even included rock guitar on one of the songs on our new album!

It must be a great feeling to get good reviews, but do you ever find it hard to cope with criticism?
Constructive criticism is one thing, but sometimes people are just nasty for the sake of it, and then it's best to turn a blind eye. You get hardened to it after a while. You can't escape criticism as we're in the public eye, but if you let it get you down, it would just drive you crazy.

If you were stranded on a desert island, what three items would you take with you?
I would take my high heels, a Nintendo 3DS to keep me entertained and my boyfriend!

What would be your perfect day out with the girls?
We love a girlie day at Sanctuary Spa in Covent Garden . . . we always go there together.

Are you a romantic?
Definitely! I'm a total romantic – I love chocolates, flowers and all those girlie things.

So, you're throwing your dream dinner party. Which four people are you going to invite?
Other than the girls in the band, I'd have Beyoncé, Rhianna, Ne-Yo and Usher. It would be sooo cool to talk music with them all evening. Beyoncé is my biggest musical inspiration!

We know about your current jigsaw obsession – but what else do you do to chill out?
I will always find time to do a bit of shopping! I am definitely the shopaholic of the band.

What's the most memorable vid you've made?
Higher was our first vid outside Europe. It was quite quick – everything came together. Everyone was on good form. It was the best time! We did some sightseeing and it all felt quite casual. It was more about having a laugh!

If you weren't in The Saturdays what would you be doing?
I can't imagine doing anything else except singing and dancing, but I'd love to settle down and have a family one day.

How do you feel about the first-ever official Saturdays annual?
I LOVE that we've got an annual! I used to love getting an annual at Christmas so this is really exciting!

> "I'd love to settle down and have a family one day."

Style File: Frankie

Must-have beauty items
• Make-up remover – the slap has to come off ASAP after a show or night out!
• It's a bit random but hairclips are a must, all the products on your hair mean that if your hair's on your forehead it can give you spots.
• Mascara. I like dark eyes with long lashes.

Top Fashion Tip
Don't look too 'try hard'. I prefer to look simply thrown together and effortless.

Top Beauty Tip
Try new things. It takes a while to get it right but you don't know unless you try. This is especially true with hair. You've got to be daring and give it a chop. I always think – 'Just do it – it'll grow back!'

Top Hair Tip
Use wax to give texture and hairspray to hold it.

Top Health Tip
Eat at healthily as you can, but if you want something just have it. I love cheeseburgers and if I want one I'll always have one.

Exercise Routine
I don't do as much exercise as I used to, but we're constantly busy and can get away with it. I have just started Pilates. I prefer classes because I get bored standing on a machine.

Frankie's Style-bites
• My fave high street shop is Zara. Their blazers fit well and their clothes are affordable but always look expensive.
• My trademark look is a vest top, jeans and heels. If you can rock that you can work any look.
• My fave designer is BCBG. I've got loads of their stuff. I love the fact they do a good range of sizes.
• I never use conditioner, because my hair is short and doesn't need it and I have shiny hair anyway. I was blonde for a while and I did actually find I had more fun. I went out a lot! But in the end I prefer my natural colour and I'm flying the flag for brunettes. Brown hair is gorgeous!

Mollie's Style-bites
• I have to wash my hair every day or it looks greasy. I'm so jealous of Rochelle – she does hers about once a week and it looks fab.
• I love playing sports – I'm not allowed to ski any more in case I break a bone. But I sometimes waterski. I'm pretty active even on my days off.

Style File: Mollie

Must-have beauty items
• Illuminating concealer for under my eyes.
• Anything from Decleor including their cleanser.
• My eyelash curlers.

Top Fashion Tip
I love the big sunglasses look!

Top Beauty Tip
If you've got a blemish don't overdo the concealer – that makes it more obvious. Just live with it and put on a smile to distract from your zit.

Top Hair Tip
Use curling tongs for a loose wave on your hair or try big rollers at the roots just to give yourself volume. When you don't have a night out planned then give it a break by just rough-drying it quickly or leaving it to dry on its own.

Top Health Tip
Cut out the junk food.

Exercise Routine
I work out few times a week with my friend Natalie at Bodyism, which is a personal training company. She helps me with my weak knees.

Style File: Una

Must-have beauty items
- Good foundation
- Lipgloss
- Mascara

Top Fashion Tip
Team a simple dress with colourful shoes for a head-turning look.

Top Beauty Tip
Always match your neck with your face. Don't forget to blend your fake tan or foundation!

Top Hair Tip
Give your hair treatments whenever you can. The best treatment is to let your hair get greasy (sounds disgusting but it works). I have to wash it when I'm working and the more I do, the greasier it gets. It's a vicious circle. The natural oils are great for it so step away from the products and go au naturel!

Top Health Tip
Go for power walks with your BFFs and shape up as you share the goss.

Exercise Routine
I don't get to swim much now. As I swam competitively I find it hard to relax when I swim – I start sprinting up and down. I used to be a gym bunny but I don't have a membership now as I wouldn't get the use of it, so I rely on dancing to keep me fit at the minute.

Una's Style-bites
- I've never gone out without make-up. Ever. The least I'll have on is tinted moisturiser. I feel raw without it.
- I have a helping hand with colour as I'm naturally a chestnut brown shade.
- I absolutely hate shopping coz I can't bear trying things on, so I love shopping online at sites like ASOS. It's a one-stop shop and I love that you can see the models wearing stuff.
- The designer stuff I have is mainly shoes and sunglasses. Everything else is high street.
- I'm a glasses junkie – I have some Tom Ford ones and D & G and Versace and Prada . . . see what I mean?

Style File: Vanessa

Must-have beauty items
• Bronzing powder
• Bright lipstick – pink, orange and red are my current faves.
• A pair of false lashes – I'm a pro at putting them on now because I've got so used to it on shoots.

Top Fashion Tip
Accept that you will make fashion mistakes along the way!

Top Beauty Tip
Beauty is all about being individual. Don't follow trends, just choose stuff that suits you and accentuates your features.

Top Hair Tip
Don't style your hair too much – it can really dry out.

Top Health Tip
Never miss out on breakfast!

Exercise Routine
I love running. I also quite like biking. I didn't do sports at school; I did dance. When I was younger I did sprinting. People didn't think I could run fast as I am short, so I used to surprise everyone.

Vanessa's Style-bites
• I am really interested in make-up. I love making myself up, it's a hobby.
• My hair is very curly and it frizzes up in the rain.
• I have changed my hair so much! I had long dark hair, then cut it. I've been red, blonde and purple. Now I'm back to what I was originally and I'm sticking to that.
• My fave high street shop is Urban Outfitters.
• I'm a huge accessories and a big bag person. I bought a Balenciaga recently. My bags have their own compartment in my wardrobe.

Style File: Rochelle

Must-have beauty items
- Foundation
- Mascara
- Cream blushers

Top Fashion Tip
Find out what works for you and stick with it!

Top Beauty Tip
Cream blusher works on cheeks and lips to give you a peachy look.

Top Hair Tip
They say you should have regular trims to help your hair grow, but I always make the mistake of chopping too much off. So if you get easily bored get yourself some extensions or a wig – that way you can change your look without regretting it!

Top Health Tip
Drink loads of water, I feel better when I do, but I don't do it enough. I'm going to try harder to remember though!

Exercise Routine
We dance a lot in rehearsals and shows and TV appearances. That's fine. I don't want to be doing anything else.

Rochelle's Style-bites
- I always fancy a bob in winter and then after two weeks I'm sick of it and spend months trying to grow it out. I've told my hairdresser to refuse to do it the next time I ask him and to just buy me a bob wig.
- My fave high street shops are Zara and Urban Outfitters.
- I love Louboutin shoes and Herve Leger bandeau dresses, they're now my signature thing! The magazines are always saying 'Will she ever step out of her comfort zone?' I practically have one in every colour.

Frankie
Mollie
Una
Vanessa
Rochelle
Whatcha
doing
Saturday
girl?

QUIZ PART 5 – TOP TWEETS

The Saturdays are Twitter crazy! Read the tweets below. Can you guess which girl tweeted them?

1. Lord please protect my body from what I have eaten today, Amen!'

2. 'I had a really weird dream that I had a pet baby Rhino the size of a kitten, it kept biting my fingers and running away… How random!'

3. 'In our hotel room getting ready, as you can imagine it's a tip in here, food, nail polish, heels, dresses, make up – chaos!!!'

4. 'Thinking too much about getting Britney tickets that I've spilt chocolate croissant all down my top!'

5. 'Meeting time!!! I've gone for a dress today because its sunny . . . I think it may have fooled me slightly . . . it's not that warm! Whoops!'

6. 'I bought new covers and pillows for my bed, they are really colourful! Makes me happy just looking at them :)'

7. 'Potatoooo.'

8. 'Steaming my head at the hairdressers! Lol.'

9. 'Coffee coffee coffee!'

10. Uh huh you know what it is, queen in yellow, queen in yellow, queen in yellow, queen in yellow! Ahhh hahahahaha! Amazing!'

TEAM SATS HIGHLIGHTS OF 2011

So what made 2011 the best year ever for Team Sats? Grab a mug of tea and a bar of chocolate and join them as they spill their secrets!

"Releasing tour dates for the arena tour. It was a massive dream to do an arena tour so I feel I've ticked that box." *Frankie*

"The day we saw our new album cover was so exciting! I think it's the best so far." *Mollie*

"Writing our album. We'd only done B-sides before and now we've penned some album tracks. For a band that's quite an important creative step." *Frankie*

"Winning our Glamour Award! We won best band – it was the first award we've won and we were sooo excited. There were so many stars in the audience. We met Kim Kardashian and Davina McCall . . . we couldn't believe it. I said the acceptance speech and all I could think was 'Don't mess it up cause you're speaking on behalf of all the girls.' When we went backstage we let out the biggest scream!" *Mollie*

"Shooting 'Notorious' was really amazing. It was our second time in L.A. and we were out there for a week again, but this time we kind of knew our way around. We did sightseeing and hung out. It was fab!" *Mollie*

"I've loved our trips to L.A.!" *Vanessa*

"This year's been action packed – we've done so much. We'll have completed two tours at each end of this year, which is a massive achievement. We've written tracks ourselves on our new album so we have put a lot in. Tours are massive memories. They've been a great way to start and end the year." *Una*

"Doing the festivals! Being on the same bill as The Script was a highlight for me as I'm a big fan. I watched them perform and all the fans were finishing off the lyrics." *Una*

We love making lists – here's some of our favourite songs, sayings and more from the past year!

TOP TUNES OF 2011

1. Beyonce – Best Thing I Never Had
2. Loick Essien – How I Roll
3. Olly Murs – Heart Skips A Beat
4. Adele – Set Fire To The Rain
5. Wretch 32 – Don't Go
6. Dev – Bass Down Low
7. Ed Sheeran – The A Team
8. JLS – She Makes Me Wanna
9. Aloe Blacc – I Need A Dollar
10. Adele – Someone Like You

FAVE MUSIC VIDEOS OF 2011

1. Jennifer Lopez – I'm Into You
2. Beyonce – Run The World (Girls)
3. Chris Brown & Justin Bieber – Next To You
4. Britney Spears – Till The World Ends
5. One Direction – What Makes You Beautiful
6. Cover Drive – Lick Ya Down
7. Lil Wayne – How To Love
8. Eminem & Rihanna – Love The Way You Lie
9. The Saturdays – All Fired Up
10. Rihanna – Only Girl (In The World)

FAVE ALBUMS OF 2011

1. Rihanna - Loud
2. Beyonce – 4
3. Adele – 21
4. Bruno Mars - Doo–Wops and Hooligans
5. Britney Spears – Femme Fatale
6. Chris Brown - F.A.M.E
7. Tinie Tempah - Disc-Overy
8. Wretch 32 – Black & White
9. Jessie J – Who You Are
10. Katy Perry – Teenage Dream

TOP THINGS TO DO ON A SATURDAY

1. Watching DVDs with friends
2. Having a girlie spa day
3. Going for a country walk with the dogs
4. Cooking up a feast with some mates
5. Going out dancing
6. Pyjama party
7. Shopping
8. Hanging with the family
9. Bike rides
10. Catching up with friends on the phone

FAVOURITE MOMENTS FROM THE 'HEADLINES' TOUR

1. Performing for our families and friends in London
2. Filming our series 'What Goes On Tour' for Channel 4
3. Seeing our stage for the first time in production rehearsals in Rhyl
4. Hanging out with our awesome musicians and crew after coming off stage every night
5. Travelling to cities we've never seen before
6. Our acoustic section where we sang 'Died In Your Eyes'
7. Una getting to perform at home in Ireland
8. Finding time for a bit of shopping
9. Singing our Rihanna medley – we're such fans
10. Our final night party!!

MOST OVERHEARD FROM THE SATS

1. Oh stop it! - Vanessa
2. Cookie monster!! -Frankie
3. I'm on the phone to my mother –Una
4. I'll be there in 5 minutes –Mollie
5. I know it's April, but I'm off to do my Christmas shopping -Rochelle
6. I love a cup of tea, me! -Una
7. I didn't MEAN to go out, it just happened! -Vanessa
8. I'm hungry – when are we eating? - Mollie
9. Eughh, what's that smell? -Rochelle
10. Awesome! -Frankie

Connect with The Saturdays and other members of Team Sats online!

Visit us at http://www.thesaturdays.co.uk for all the latest news, tour dates, music videos and our weekly online TV show 'All Fired Up At…'

twitter

Follow us on Twitter at @TheSaturdays @FrankieTheSats @MollieTheSats @RochelleTheSats @VanessaWhite @UnaHealy

facebook

Like us on Facebook at
http://www.facebook.com/TheSaturdays
http://www.facebook.com/FrankieTheSaturdays
http://www.facebook.com/MollieTheSaturdays
http://www.facebook.com/RochelleTheSaturdays
http://www.facebook.com/UnaTheSaturdays
http://www.facebook.com/VanessaTheSaturdays

WHAT'S NEXT...

We really hope you've enjoyed reading our annual!

Right now while writing this letter, we're in the middle of preparing for our 'All Fired Up' arena tour. It's going to be our biggest and best tour yet – don't miss it! We'll be performing all our hits, some of our new tracks plus some massive surprises.

We're also about to release our brand-new album 'On Your Radar' which we're SO proud of. We've written half the tracks ourselves, so it's a bit nerve-wracking unleashing them on the public. We really hope you like them! We'll of course be reading what the press have to say – but we also can't wait to hear your thoughts on our forum, Twitter and Facebook. Make sure you let us know which tracks are your favourites!

Next year, we plan to release another single from the album, which means filming a new video, shooting the artwork, creating some new choreography and getting out on the promo trail.

We also hope to release a record in Europe or America – and collaborate with some new artists, writers and producers. Our dream would be to do a world tour – visiting all the places we've never been before.

2012 going to be an AMAZING year for the Sats. Hope you'll all be along for the ride!

Love,

Frankie, Mollie, Una, Vanessa and Rochelle xx

It's the moment of truth . . .
just how much do you know about The Saturdays? Time to tot up your score and face the music.

10–20 OK, you need to do your homework! There is a whole glorious world of pop out there for you to explor

21–35 Good work. Perhaps not a Saturdays anorak, but you know what you're talking about!

36–50 Wow! You really know your stuff. Gold star.

Pages 22-23
Quiz Part 1
Test Yourself!
1. Chasing Lights
2. Just Can't Get Enough
3. Una
4. Fascination Records
5. JLS
6. Una
7. Depeche Mode
8. Flo Rida
9. The Saturdays 24/7
10. Rochelle

Pages 38-39
Quiz Part 2
It's All In the Lyrics
1. Higher
2. Up
3. Notorious
4. Work
5. If this is Love
6. Ego
7. Issues
8. Just Can't Get Enough
9. Missing you
10. Forever is Over

Pages 50-51
Quiz Part 3
Moving Pictures
1. Notorious
2. Higher
3. Ego
4. Work
5. Missing You
6. Issues
7. Up
8. Just Can't Get Enough
9. Forever is Over
10. If This Is Love

Total Score

Pages 70-71
Quiz Part 4
Back to Their Roots
1. Mollie
2. Mollie
3. Una
4. Mollie
5. Mollie
6. Vanessa
7. Frankie and Rochelle
8. Una
9. Frankie
10. Vanessa

Pages 82-83
Quiz Part 5
Top Tweets
1. Rochelle
2. Una
3. Rochelle
4. Mollie
5. Frankie
6. Una
7. Frankie
8. Una
9. Vanessa
10. Mollie

Pages 40

```
V A N E S S A R O M O D R U S
I U R O C A V E L Y T S Y A N
D E C I S T Y L R D O M T U O
E S E L L U F G A N U U M N T
O U R E H R U N S S R O D T R
S A K O A D I L E D S S U R I
A M O D R A T S V E T S N D O
T D E R O Y D A I G M O A U
O I D U T S T K D E O T Y S
M S O N O N L L H E K A J
I S M A N A V I S R H L S S A
D U A S R N T M O L L I E T R
E E O F O D R A T M A T O U
O S U K C V A N E S A R K M V
S A S E R O C H E L L E T S I
```

Pages 72-72

```
        F
HIGHER  R
   O   VANESSA    A
   M   A       L LIONKING
   U   N       F
MU     K       I        N
MOLLIE E    U  R        A
            N  C A P R I C O R N
SHORTIE     A  E        G
  H         N  D        H
BEYONCE     E    W      T
  O              H      Y
  P I N K    D I V E R S I T Y
  I             T      T
RYANHOPE        E      H
                       E
                       S
                DISNEY C
                       R
                       I
                       P
                       T
```